nordic wisdom

nordic wisdom

simplify your life and
cultivate well-being

elisabeth carlsson

CICO BOOKS

Published in 2025 by CICO Books
An imprint of Ryland Peters & Small Ltd

20–21 Jockey's Fields
London WC1R 4BW

1452 Davis Bugg Road
Warrenton, NC 27589

www.rylandpeters.com
Email: euregulations@rylandpeters.com

10 9 8 7 6 5 4 3 2 1

Some of the text in this book first appeared in *The Book of Nordic Self-Care*, *The Lagom Life*, *The Green Cure*, and *A Year of Living Happily*.

Text © Elisabeth Carlsson 2017, 2024, 2025
Text on page 110–111 © Alice Peck 2019, 2025
Text on 124–125 © Lois Blyth 2017, 2025
Design © CICO Books 2025
See page 143 for picture credits

The author's moral rights have been asserted. All rights reserved. No part of this publication may be reproduced, stored in a retrieval system, or transmitted in any form or by any means, electronic, mechanical, photocopying, or otherwise, without the prior permission of the publisher.

A CIP record for this book is available from the British Library.
US Library of Congress CIP data has been applied for.

ISBN: 978-1-80065-454-9

Printed in China

Designer: Geoff Borin
Assistant editor: Danielle Rawlings
Art director: Sally Powell
Senior designer: Emily Breen
Head of production: Patricia Harrington
Creative director: Leslie Harrington
Publishing manager: Carmel Edmonds

The authorised representative in the EEA is Authorised Rep Compliance Ltd., Ground Floor, 71 Lower Baggot Street, Dublin, D01 P593, Ireland
www.arccompliance.com

Safety note:

Neither the author nor the publisher can be held responsible for any claim arising out of the general information provided in this book. Please note that while particular practices refer to healing benefits, they are not intended to replace a diagnosis of illness or ailments, or healing or medicine. Always consult your doctor or other health professional in the case of illness. The safe and proper use of candles is the sole responsibility of the person using them. Do not leave a burning candle unattended. Never burn a candle on or near anything that might catch fire. Keep candles out of the reach of children and pets.

contents

introduction 6

chapter 1
nordic values 10

chapter 2
the nordic connection to nature 32

chapter 3
the nordic home 76

chapter 4
a nordic lifestyle 112

conclusion 138

resources 142
picture credits 143
acknowledgments 144

introduction

This is a book about the Nordic countries, their people, and their lifestyle. It's also about the life lessons I learned from growing up in Sweden and, as so often is the way, only seeing the true value of that when other distractions lost their shine.

The Nordic countries include Denmark, Finland, Norway, Sweden, Greenland, the autonomous region of Finland called Åland, and the Faroe Islands, a self-governing administrative overseas region of Denmark. Life there is a lot about the small joys—not insignificant things but simple luxuries that don't cost a lot, such as going out for that daily walk in the park, loving nature in all its forms, creating a simple soup from seasonal ingredients without having to look at a recipe, decluttering a drawer, snuggling up with a soft wool blanket, and having your morning cup of tea outside while feeling the earth under your feet.

"The world is a series of miracles, but we're so used to them we call them ordinary things."

Hans Christian Andersen, Danish author

appreciating the world around you

Living well in the Nordic countries is also about learning to love nature in all its forms and knowing that a deep connection to the landscape has an impact on your well-being. Finding a way of appreciating nature every day, whether you live in an urban environment or the countryside, is essential, and this book includes tips on how to do this. Living in line with the natural world, whether through food, celebrations, planting seeds and watching them grow, bringing a flask of tea and something to eat outdoors, immersing yourself in natural waters, or having the scent from spring flowers wafting throughout your house can all form part of an intention to live a healthier, happier, and simpler life.

chapter 1

nordic values

finding balance

The Nordic countries usually come in the top five happiest countries of the World Happiness Report. There are lots of reasons for this, but one of them is the ideas and values that these countries share.

Sweden, in particular, is often described as the ultimate model, where things are done right—gender equality, social security, and quality of life lead to happiness. Even though Swedish society has changed a lot in recent decades, as has society in most other countries, Sweden still feels like a country with a culture that is geared toward people. Putting people first comes from a *lagom* attitude—achieving the balance between working hard and having time for the rest of your community and family.

Lagom is more of a philosophy than a lifestyle, a central approach to life that says everyone can have a piece of the pie—and exactly the right piece—just in a *lagom* amount. It's a kind of Swedish Goldilocks approach, with everything "just right." But you don't have to live in Sweden to practice this sort of attitude and boost your happiness and contentment.

finding balance **13**

lagom

"lah-gom" • **Swedish** • **noun**
The philosophy of living a balanced, moderately paced, low-fuss life—not too much of something, not too little, but just right.

the nordic approach to life

The Nordics take their time to do things right. At work they will set aside tasks to have regular breaks for *fika* (see page 116) together, not alone. The Norwegians regularly take Friday afternoons off to enjoy their *friluftsliv* (see page 42) and a recent four-day working week trial in Iceland was a big success, showing that productivity stayed the same. The Nordic countries seem to have nailed that elusive goal of a good work/life balance mainly because they have normalized flexible and remote working.

The Nordics also take time to do things they enjoy in an uncomplicated way, and celebrations such as Christmas, Midsummer, and Easter are usually low key with a strong focus on being together with family or friends. When you find a balanced way to do things, they become more manageable and you can take the pressure off yourself and others too. And weirdly, when you take things slow, you actually gain more time.

the nordic approach to life 17

keep things simple

Surround yourself with nice things but don't fall into that trap of believing that spending money on stuff makes you happy. We've all been there in IKEA, coming out with another Pärkla storage case instead of decluttering. There is a fine line in between taking up a new hobby and buying an excessive amount of gear for it, so aim for the sensible *lagom* (see page 14) approach here. Focus more on unpretentious moments spent with friends and family, and creating *hygge* (see page 80) with simple things such as cooking uncomplicated food together or even outdoors, perhaps accompanied by a fire or lots of candles.

think of your community

The Nordic countries also tend to prioritize the collective rather than the individual—this is known as the law of Jante (also known as *Jantelagen* in Swedish, *Janti laki* in Finnish, *Jantelögin* in Iceland, and *Janteloven* in Norwegian and Danish). There are some negative aspects to this, as the emphasis on conformity rather than individuality can lead to a general disapproval of anyone who stands out from the collective. However, we can't deny that this focus on the collective has helped to shape the success of Nordic societies.

For example, Nordic workplaces are designed to be communal and social environments, with shared spaces in offices allowing for more creativity and opportunities for workers to be seen and heard in their teams.

the nordic approach to life 21

the nordic work/life balance

Besides the flexitime and five weeks' annual vacation, Swedes also have a fair share of public holidays, or red days as they like to call them (because they are marked in red on the calendar). Red days add up to about two weeks' extra time off. If you're lucky, your employer may give you an extra half day before the red day, just to get you in the mood, and if a red day falls on a Thursday, the company may give you a *klämdag*, which basically means a squeezed day, the one in between the red day and the weekend. That day might as well not exist on the work calendar.

An American website on how to do business in Sweden advises that foreign partners should not expect to meet their Swedish counterparts after 4pm on weekdays since 5pm is going home time, and not to schedule meetings in June, July, or August or late February through March because these are popular times to go on vacation.

You do have to wonder how Swedes actually get any work done. The thing is, we Swedes really value that work/life balance, and work hard to achieve it. At work, and in many situations in life, we focus on what has to be done rather than doing unnecessary things that can eat into our leisure time.

22 nordic values

reclaim your time

While it's all very well hearing about the Swedish system, how can you achieve a decent work/life balance when you don't have five weeks' vacation, or more red days than the average American has in annual leave, or even *vabba* (time off to be with sick children)? You might think that you are not able to change anything about an office culture in which we are encouraged to work long hours.

However, think about the time that you do have that is just your own, and start by reclaiming more of that. Log out from your computer to leave the office on time. Don't have email or social-media notifications on your phone, and switch it off when you are with your family (if your kids will let you, that is). Set specific work hours and ignore any correspondence outside of those hours. You will probably find that you are just as efficient as before but you will be living a much more balanced life.

sisu

"*see-soo*" • **Finnish** • **noun**
An attitude of courage, resilience, grit, tenacity, and perseverance in the face of adversity; an integral element of Finnish culture.

þetta reddast

"*teh-ta-red-ahst*" • **Icelandic** • **phrase**
A reassurance that everything will work out all right in the end, so keep going and never give up. Literally, "it will save itself" or "it will fix itself."

the nordic approach to adversity

It's always interesting to know how other countries deal with adversity, and in recent years there has been quite a lot written about the Finnish concept of *sisu*, which can be summed up as extraordinary perseverance or, as some people call it, "the Finnish grit."

In November 1939, Russia declared war on Finland. Eight hundred thousand Finnish soldiers had to defend against two million Russian soldiers, and the confrontation between them is one of the most fascinating in history. The Finns resisted stoically, which strengthened this idea of *sisu*; the potential you have inside. The concept of *sisu* historically goes back 500 years or more but nevertheless, this is a good story to describe it.

Many of the other Nordic countries have similar concepts. Thorgerdur (or *Þorgerður* in the Icelandic spelling) Anna Gunnarsdóttir, Political and Communications Officer at the Icelandic Embassy in London says, "We have survived centuries in that barely inhabitable place so we can do anything. We really believe in ourselves."

practice resilience

All humans have this potential dormant inside of them. Adversity awakens it in us, when we use it to resist, overcome, and persist. Some of the lessons you can take from *sisu* are to control stress and not let fear dominate you. Perseverance is a trait in decline as most of us are impatient and want things right now, but as the old saying goes, good things come to those who wait.

However, be mindful and know when to ask for help. Tiina Knuuttiila, a program manager from Finland now living in Spain, says that "*sisu* is an integral part of one's self-worth, I must be able to be strong and resilient for that is what I am. But on the flipside it's a sense of duty and independence and not asking for help, because if I do then I owe them and hence it is not really free." As well as *sisu*, make sure that you practice simple self-care so you can in turn look after other people too and ask for help yourself.

the nordic approach to adversity

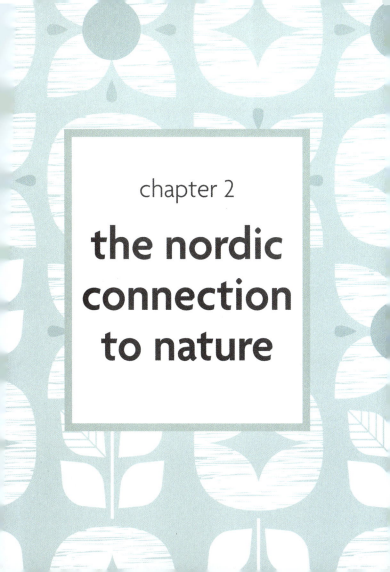

chapter 2

the nordic connection to nature

a deep love for the great outdoors

The Nordic countries often conjure up images of clean, untouched, and undisturbed natural landscapes with few people—the deep forests and lakes of Sweden and Finland, the windswept beaches of Denmark and Åland, and the rugged mountains of Iceland, the Faroe Islands, and Norway.

Nature is deeply rooted in the Nordic soul, and the people of these countries have long lived in tandem with their environment. All the Nordic countries have stories of mythical creatures such as elves and trolls, which are told to children from an early age, giving them a respect and pride in their environment as well as a desire to protect the natural world.

It doesn't come as a surprise then that a love of spending time outdoors is one of the things that the Nordics have in common.

the nordic view of nature

The saying "there is no bad weather, only bad clothing" is a maxim all Nordics live by, because if they were worried about a bit of rain, snow, and cold then they wouldn't go out for about six months of the year. Not being preoccupied by the weather can be very liberating—you just get dressed for the occasion and get out.

The Nordics know that spending time in nature is beneficial on so many levels, so there really isn't a debate about if the weather fits an outing or not. "It's all about the mindset and it doesn't take much to shift your thinking about weather," says Kari Leibowitz, a PhD student at Stanford University who spent a year in Tromsø, north of the Arctic Circle. She discovered that the Norwegians had "a positive winter mindset," embracing the dark season and turning it into something *koselig* (see page 129).

In fact, the Nordics have a long tradition of outdoor childcare provisions, and outdoor time is part of the curriculum in these countries. Norway has several outdoor kindergartens or *friluftsbarnehager*, and in Sweden, *Skogsmulle* (a method of teaching through outdoor learning activities) has provided nature-based education for children since the 1950s.

the nordic view of nature

change up your environment

Spending time in nature is a big contributor to well-being. Research has shown over and over again how spending time in natural surroundings impacts our mood, reduces our stress levels, and can improve how your nervous and immune systems as well as endocrine system (which is made up of glands that produce hormones) are working.

While you can't always get outside, studies show that even a single plant in an office, hospital, or school can have a significant beneficial impact, and research from Helsinki University found that kids who swapped gravel and concrete to play on with a forest-based playground, improved their immunity in only a week. Children playing outside generally fight less, have fewer tantrums, and usually cooperate well.

connect with the outdoors

There is something in nature that resonates with humans, making us feel calm and as though we are coming home. Perhaps we are part of nature, not separate from it like the philosopher Descartes suggested.

Forest bathing, or *shinrin yoku*, is a concept that emerged in Japan in 1908 and means being in the forest, breathing deeply, and taking in the atmosphere. "Touching trees reinforces the idea that we are at one with nature," says Dr. Miles Richardson, a nature connection psychologist and the author of the book *Reconnected*. "That connection, in turn, has been linked to things like greater life expectancy, a higher sense of 'meaningfulness,' lower cognitive anxiety, and better body image."

This has given rise to practices such as forest medicine and "eco therapy" (which involves doing activities in nature). Forest bathing is the science of using nature to heal yourself. The Nordics don't need a term like *shinrin yoku* to back up what they have known forever though: that being in nature makes you feel better.

the nordic view of nature **41**

friluftsliv

"free-loofts-liv" • **Norwegian** • **noun**
The act of spending time in outdoor locations to enhance one's spiritual and physical well-being. Literally, "free air life."

the importance of nature in society

The term *friluftsliv* was popularized in the 1850s by the Norwegian playwright and poet, Henrik Ibsen, who used it in a poem to explain the experience of being immersed in nature and how that is related to a person's spiritual and physical growth.

In 2009–11, Nordic outdoor organizations ran the joint project *Frisk I Naturen* (Health in Nature). It sought to gather knowledge around what nature and *friluftsliv* can do for health, and put it high on the political agenda and in the hands of decision makers in society. It also aimed to give this knowledge to people working in health and nature sectors, so that they could apply it in their work. The connection between nature and health could then be reinforced by health-care workers, landscape gardeners, and city planners.

The positive effect nature has on mental health was clear from the project's extensive report—even a short time of only 4–5 minutes spent in nature was proven to be beneficial. So green areas and playgrounds in urban areas are key for reducing people's stress and preventing so many of the illnesses we just think are part and parcel of a modern lifestyle.

do what you can to get out

Globally, 56.2 percent of the population now lives in cities, so most of us don't have a nearby mountain to climb or an uninterrupted view of a valley. However, *friluftsliv* is not connected to a specific activity—you don't need to strap on your skis or travel to a remote area—you can just make the best of the opportunities you have.

The daily practice of seeking out nature where you are is more important than doing a wild trek once a year. The Swedish-American writer Linda Åkeson McGurk, author of the book *The Open Air Life*, says that "setting an intention to get out in nature is key to actually finding a practice which then becomes part of the fabric of your life."

Make a "date" with the outside world—schedule it in your diary if that is what it takes. Seek out activities that include an outdoor element, find something that you enjoy, and embrace the weather whatever the season.

stop and smell the roses

Humans aren't really built for our modern lifestyle. Homo sapiens have lived on earth for at least 50,000 years and our biology has only changed about 0.003 percent since the ice age, which lasted until 11,500 years ago. It's not surprising that the speed that characterizes today's society has a detrimental effect on our mental health. We are constantly switched on, and every minute of the day is planned with activities where nature simply does not fit in.

As an antidote to this, across the Nordic region, nature or garden therapy is readily available on the health service for burnout, chronic fatigue, and PTSD (post-traumatic stress discorder). At Alnarp University of Agricultural Sciences in Sweden, they have had a rehabilitation or healing garden since 2002, where it has been demonstrated again and again how surrounding yourself with plants can be more effective than using medication.

Try taking a slow walk in your nearby city park as a way of including *friluftsliv* in your self-care practice. It is not about competition and achievement, it's more about choosing nature to be part of your life. You go from a state of doing to a state of just being.

the importance of nature in society **49**

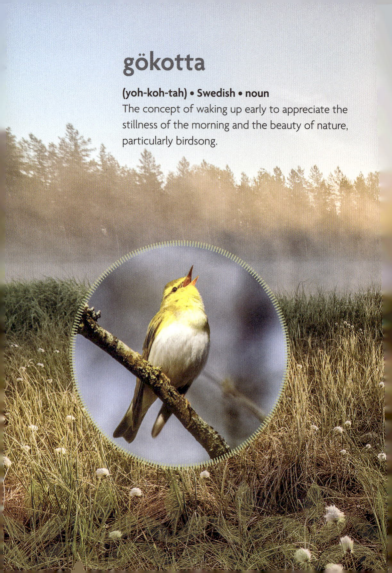

gökotta

(yoh-koh-tah) • Swedish • noun
The concept of waking up early to appreciate the stillness of the morning and the beauty of nature, particularly birdsong.

the nordic approach to exercise

We all find it pretty hard to get out there and exercise regularly, but the Nordics don't seem to have this problem so much. I can guarantee that if you chat to a Swede the conversation will eventually lead to them telling you about what they do for exercise or their latest health interest or outdoor pursuit.

With the rise of consumerist individualism in other countries, the popularity of outdoor exercise has arguably suffered. Although, according to 2022 data from the Eurobarometer, which conducts surveys on behalf of the European Commission, the Nordic countries have the lowest value of non-exercising people, with just 8 percent in Finland, 12 percent in Sweden, and 20 percent in Denmark, compared to 23 percent in Germany and 45 percent in France.

Some think the Nordic penchant for outdoor activities is related to the values of puritanical Lutheranism, which have historically been especially influential in Sweden and Norway. However, the high levels of people doing sporty activities outdoors in the Nordic countries probably also have something to do with the importance they place on being in nature.

take your workout outside

Outdoor exercise is widely believed to build character, and children from a young age in the Nordic countries are used to doing outdoor activities to boost fitness and resilience. The half-term school holidays in Sweden are even called *sportlov*, sporting holidays, which tells you all you need to know really. I remember orienteering fondly from my school days mainly because we were running around in the woods and could take cheeky breaks behind a pine tree.

"For individuals who have not exercised for many years, the forest is a place with a low threshold," says Kati Vähäsarja, who ran Moved by Nature, a Finnish project promoting exercise in nature. Not only is it free or inexpensive, but it has so many brilliant advantages other than fitness.

the nordic approach to exercise **55**

keep it simple

Being present, connecting with nature by practicing *friluftsliv* (see page 42), and staying active without pushing yourself in a gym is usually the Nordic approach to fitness. As with anything, the Nordics keep it simple, sustainable, and naturally sourced.

Research has shown that minimal movement is better than none, so just some gentle walking or even gardening can help. Often, we get put off because we link exercise with the idea of losing weight, and lots of people have negative associations with this which is understandable. However, exercise has numerous benefits that have nothing to do with stepping on a scale. For example, it improves cognitive function and makes your thinking sharper, as it stimulates the production of new brain cells.

My son is a prime example of this as when he started exercising and strength training in his last year of high school, his memory and grades improved and his teachers asked if he was the same boy. Movement is also protective against aging of the brain, as it increases the size of the hippocampus, which controls short-term memory.

nordic outdoor activities to try

Linda Åkeson McGurk (see page 46) says that when you have spent a large part of your day inside there is a fundamental need to get out of the house. *"Nu måste vi komma ut"* is another mantra I grew up with and means simply that you just have to get outside; it's a way to reset your mood and stops your thoughts from going into overdrive.

Deep down we know that connecting with nature is good for us, but if this is not something we grew up with, we might not actively choose it. Some ways that Nordic people connect with nature are through wild swimming, hiking, foraging, and visiting a sauna—see if any of these resonate with you.

nordic outdoor activities to try 59

wild swimming

If you fancy a swim in the Nordic countries, you are never far from a lake, the sea, or, if you are in Iceland, a hot spring. Growing up in Sweden, I learned to swim in the summer holidays by going to a swimming school that was held for six weeks at my local lake, come rain or shine. Because the school began at the end of June, the lake hadn't quite warmed up yet so it was common to swim in water that was 60–65°F (15–18°C).

Wild swimming, especially in the winter months, is a trend that has been slowly becoming more mainstream outside of the Nordic countries. Although no one in the Nordic countries would ever call it "wild" swimming—to us, it's just swimming. The Nordics have always had a tradition of swimming outdoors, and the health benefits of this practice are numerous.

If you feel that winter and the dark weather are getting you down, wild swimming might help get you through this season and be a self-care practice that lifts you up and empowers you. Of course, you can also try this in the summer and gradually work your way toward swimming in colder temperatures through the fall and winter.

Only go wild swimming if you're in good health, join a local outdoor swimming group (who will know the best and safest places to swim), and never go alone.

nordic outdoor activities to try **61**

hiking

In most of the Nordic countries, the freedom to roam is seen as a right—*allmansrätten* in Swedish, *friluftsloven* in Norwegian, and *jokamiehen oikeudet* in Finnish. This, plus the Nordic connection to nature, means hiking is a popular pastime. In fact, hiking is so commonplace in Norway, it's not unusual to use it for a first date.

Getting outdoors is an excellent form of self-care as you always feel better afterward, but it really helps to have the right kit. The saying "there is no such thing as bad weather, only bad clothing," comes to mind. If you are uncomfortable or get cold or wet, the great outdoors doesn't seem so great anymore.

Think three layers—a base layer that helps with moisture control, a warm reinforcement layer, and a waterproof outside layer for the winter months. If you are into longer treks, your most important purchase will be your shoes, because no one wants to think about sore and uncomfortable feet. I think it's also worth buying socks that are meant for hiking as they have the right grip.

64 the nordic connection to nature

foraging

A strong memory from my childhood is hours of boredom out in the woods, fighting off midges, and looking for berries. I say "boredom" because quite often what you have on your doorstep is not that interesting, especially in your teenage years. Now, I am very grateful for those experiences as they taught me to appreciate nature and seasonal foods before living in cities for the best part of my adulthood.

Living from nature is a way to be more sustainable and foraging connects you with a slow-living lifestyle. Because when you forage, you are not in a hurry. You are in contact with nature, going slowly, eyes peeled for things to add to your basket. By going at a slower pace, you breathe more calmly, you start to notice the smells and sounds in nature, and you are also focused because you have a goal.

Of course, foraging is mainly a country pursuit; not everyone has a wood nearby, and you might live in a city and worry about the pollution. However, I live in a city and I have discovered that foraging is indeed possible there too. Just behind our house in London, there is a lone plum tree, laden with fruit each year. My freezer has several bags of halved plums, ready for a pie.

Note that you should always forage with an expert as many varieties of wild mushroom and fruit can be poisonous or harmful to eat. Why not join a foraging group and meet new friends?

sauna

Visiting a sauna is a tradition that is deeply ingrained in the Finnish culture. With 3.2 million saunas in a country of 5.5 million people, it is often said that the entire Finnish population would be able to go to a sauna at the same time at any given moment.

Sauna culture involves much more than simply sitting in a wooden room enjoying the warm *löyly* (steam) and the *vihtu* (a birch branch that can be used to increase air circulation and acts as a natural form of aromatherapy). In a sauna, people cleanse both their bodies and minds and embrace a sense of inner peace. Traditionally, the sauna has been considered a sacred space—a "church of nature."

Saunas can also ease pain and aid in recovery from injury. The increased blood flow you get from the heat in the sauna helps to speed up the body's natural healing processes. Tiina Knuuttiila (see page 30) says "it was once called the 'poor man's pharmacy'... the tarring of the wood inside the sauna prompting the proverb 'if liquor, tar, and sauna won't help, an illness is fatal'."

sólarfrí

"*solar-free*" • **Icelandic** • **noun**

A "sun-vacation." Offices in Iceland are occasionally closed on sunny days so workers can enjoy the nice weather. A good reminder to appreciate sunny days.

the nordic emphasis on natural light

The Nordic countries place much significance on light. From the endless brightness in summer to the deep darkness in winter, light has become a key part of their culture. Even when the absence of sunlight is most evident, the sky sometimes lights up with the help of the northern lights.

You'll know a Nordic person as they will be the one sitting outside in the winter months, wrapped up warm, perhaps under a heat lamp, with their face aimed toward the sun as soon as it makes an appearance.

A lot of Nordic buildings are designed and built with a special focus on how to best use the scarce light in winter, as well as the light throughout the long summer days. Adapting to the seasons (see page 98) and having several light spots is important indoors, as well as maximizing the natural light coming in by avoiding covering up windows in winter.

the nordic emphasis on natural light

maximize your sunlight

Low levels of natural light can have implications on our health not only because it reduces the production of vitamin D in our bodies, but also because it affects our sleep–wake cycle and our serotonin (a hormone that helps prevents depression) and melatonin (a hormone that helps us sleep) production. There are vitamin D receptors all over the body, as well as in the heart and reproductive organs, for example—basically in a lot of places where the sun don't shine! Studies show that low levels of vitamin D play a role in SAD (Seasonal Affective Disorder), which is very common in the northernmost countries, and that increased vitamin D status lowers depressive symptoms.

If you are struggling to fit in natural light in the day, consider making some adjustments to your schedule, such as waking up a little earlier so you can expose your face to the sunrise, or taking a regular lunchtime walk. The "D-minder" app is also useful if you want to find out how much time you need to spend outdoors to get your correct amount of sunlight, including UVB rays, which stimulate vitamin D production. The app uses your location to work out your solar noon—when the sun is at its highest in the day.

supplement your health if needed

If you're still struggling to get enough sunlight, there are several other options you can try. Lamps such as the Lumie have been proven to help with SAD symptoms and the sleep cycle—just make sure that the lamp is strong enough; 10,000 lux is four times more effective than 2500 lux.

You can also take vitamin D supplements, and complement them with vitamin K for maximum vitamin D absorption. Make sure that you have enough cholesterol (saturated fat) in your diet, as it is a carrier for all fat-soluble vitamins including vitamins D and K. However, before supplementing, you should go to a health practitioner to get advice and check your vitamin D status.

the nordic emphasis on natural light

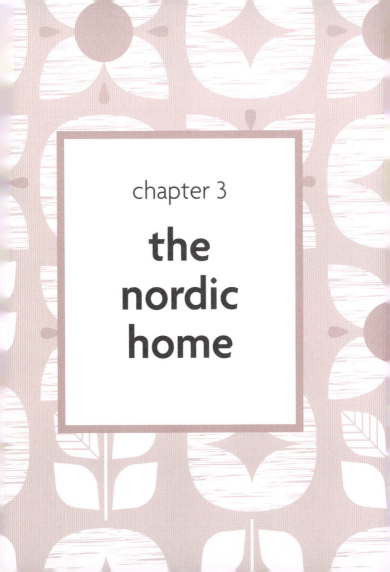

chapter 3

the nordic home

the importance of home

Creating a home that you harmonize with, where you can rest and recharge, is a key way to support your health and well-being.

Having lived in the UK for many years now, I never think that my home looks particularly Nordic, but people often comment that it has that Scandinavian feel to it. Maybe it's the fabrics, the sanded and oiled floorboards, lots of plants in every window, and of course plenty of small lamps and candles. I've actually lived abroad for longer than I have lived in Sweden now, but there are definitely core values that I grew up with that make me want to arrange my house in a certain way.

Even though my home is now a mix of all the countries I've lived in, it has got that essential Nordic touch. This chapter looks at how you can create a home that supports your own self-care, and what the Nordic way of life can teach us about it.

hygge

"hyoo-guh" • **Danish** • **noun**

An atmosphere of warmth, coziness, and contentment, where you can simply enjoy living in the moment.

nordic interior design

Nordic design emerged in the 1950s as a part of the modern movement that prioritized function and affordability over opulence and luxury. Its characteristics include natural materials, pale colors and wood, large windows to let as much light in as possible, slim features on furniture such as tapered legs on chairs, and simple lines that leave plenty of open space for an uncluttered and calm look.

Maximizing light is also very important in Nordic homes, so you won't see heavy drapes (curtains) covering the windows—instead there will be very light or no drapes. Sunlight is key to well-being; research has shown that natural light exposure in hospitals leads to patients needing less pain medication, and staff reporting feeling happier and more energetic. So maybe drop those heavy drapes.

nordic interior design **83**

simplify the décor

It doesn't matter if you are not an expert in interior decoration. Put the things that you love in pride of place, and pare back accessories and anything that doesn't fit or serve a purpose. Clever storage solutions are a priority—ideally use textured items such as wicker or wire baskets to add a natural feel. In the end, if you can keep your home uncluttered and life simpler than it was before, you can achieve more of what you want, be it time or balance.

nordic interior design

creating a warm atmosphere

One of the core principles of Nordic decorating is creating a feeling of warmth, simplicity, and coziness. The recent popularity of the Danish concept of *hygge* (see page 80) has been used to sell candles and blankets, but *hygge* is more about how to create an atmosphere that is easy to relax in. Many Nordic homes have a feeling of comfort without being overly ornate or cluttered, and incorporate just the right amount of furniture and décor. To use that other popularized Swedish word, they are *lagom* (see page 14), meaning they have just the right amount of stuff—not too much, not too little.

bring the outdoors in

Regardless of their country of origin, using nature as a feature in decorating is a key element in Nordic homes. In houses in all the Nordic countries, you will find natural colors, along with some black and white elements that reflect contrasts in nature. Other key features are natural elements such as wool, wood, and lots of plants, as well as plant designs on textiles and in the art on the walls.

döstädning

"dur-sted-ning" • **Swedish** • **noun**
The caring act of downsizing, decluttering, and organizing to make things easier for your loved ones after you pass. Literally, "death cleaning."

the nordic approach to tidiness

Not having clutter is key, as it would ruin the clean lines of Nordic design and is a major block to creating a relaxing home. Studies from both UCLA and Princeton show that clutter raises our cortisol levels and impedes our ability to problem-solve.

The curious Swedish phenomenon of *döstädning* (death cleaning) comes in here, because it focuses your mind and gives you the motivation to declutter, little by little. Margareta Magnusson coined the term after both her mother and her husband passed away within a short time of each other and she had to clear out their things, which she found exhausting and incredibly emotionally taxing. She decided to write a book about the importance of reducing your belongings so your loved ones wouldn't have to go through the same thing after your passing, which then became a bestseller the world over.

Döstädning is all about downsizing your home and belongings so that life after death can literally be lighter and easier for those who have to clear out your house. At the same time, you make your own daily life much easier, because who doesn't want less clutter? We all have so many things that we have accumulated from who knows where and don't appreciate anymore.

the nordic approach to tidiness **93**

downsize for an easier life

Döstädning doesn't have to be about death or dying though, because if you can't shut your drawers or cupboards, it's time to do something about it. It might take a while to declutter, so start adopting this as a habit instead of having one massive clear out.

One method of *döstädning* is to put things into boxes and label them so that it is clear what to do with them. You might not be ready to get rid of these things yet, but this makes it easier if someone else has to. A lot of the items we surround ourselves with have memories attached to them but what meaning do they have when they're drowning in drawers, on dusty cluttered shelves, or packed away in a cupboard? Another method is to pass an item on to someone else who might have more use for it, telling them its story so it can carry on making memories in their house.

Döstädning is a way of summarizing your life in a practical way and unearthing possessions that spark memories. Be happy about the memories that are attached to your items, and know that you don't need things to remember the fun times.

peiskos

"pise-kos" • **Norwegian** • **noun**
The feeling of well-being, warmth, and coziness achieved from sitting in front of a crackling fireplace.

living with the seasons

We all know that Nordic winters can be harsh, but what some people might not realize is how dark it is in the fall and winter. In Oslo, Norway, the sun rises around 9am and sets at about 3pm in mid-winter. Even farther north, there are only a few hours of daylight, when the light more resembles dusk. The Norwegians even have a word for this time—*mørketiden* (the dark time)—which perfectly sums it up.

The transition of the seasons can bring up emotions and increase stress levels, but using nature as a guide to help you adapt can help to lower anxiety. When you adjust to the seasons, you tune in to yourself and exactly how you are feeling. The Nordics, perhaps out of necessity, have created some key rituals around the changes of the seasons. They know how to create a home that is supportive to changes in the weather and light. As well as adapting to the harsh, cold seasons, the Nordics also make sure to celebrate the long summer nights.

spring

Spring is one of the shorter seasons but because it marks the return of the light and longer days after winter, it is something to really celebrate. Nature slowly starts to wake up again, trees are budding, and small shoots of green can be seen everywhere.

This is also the time where you can play "spot a Nordic person" as they will always find a *solglänta* or sunny corner to sit in and get those rays. After a long winter, the sun is very welcome, so never mind that the temperature is low, the Norwegians will wrap up warm to enjoy that first *utepils* (beer drunk outside) by their log cabin or *hytta*.

Use these ideas to help you make the most of this season in your home.

- **Seasonal bulbs:** Plant some flower bulbs such as pearl hyacinths or daffodils in a pot with soil and cover with moss.

- **Tree branches:** Add branches to a vase filled with water and after a few days in the warmth, they should start to bud.

- **Tulips:** Sweden's most popular flower—dot them around your home in small vases.

- **Spring display:** Create some indoor "grass" by planting rye grass seeds in a shallow dish with some soil. Decorate with mini bunnies and chicks.

- **Table decorations:** Decorate your table with a yellow tablecloth and lots of small vases of flowers and marbled eggs.

living with the seasons **101**

summer

This is when the Nordics throw open their windows and start living outside more to maximize the light and long days. Because of this, they take a lot of care to create a beautiful space outside and curate it in a way that makes them want to spend lots of time there.

This season gives us Midsummer, and while all the Nordic countries celebrate the summer solstice (the longest day of the year), the way they recognize it varies. In Denmark, it is linked to the birth of St. John the Baptist, and they call it *Sankt Hans Aften*. In Finland, Denmark, and Norway, big bonfires are lit. In Sweden it's all about the Maypole—a painted pole that's decorated with flowers, around which people traditionally dance.

102 the nordic home

decorate your outdoor space

If you have a garden or a space outside, make it into somewhere you'll want to spend as much time as possible. Decorate your patio, balcony, or garden with beautiful floral arrangements, comfortable chairs with blankets to wrap up in when the evenings get cooler, lots of outdoor candles, fairy lights, and plastic rugs on the patio.

grow scented flowers

Plant scented flowers near your patio, outdoor space, or balcony if you have one—wherever you like to sit to have your tea in the morning or glass of wine in the evening. Keep it simple by using seeds. It's a small investment with maximum return. You could try *Nicotiana sylvestris*, a plant that can grow up to 4½ foot (1.5m) tall and has a sweet fragrance that comes out in the evening, or *Cosmos*, an easy plant to grow with a long flowering season.

living with the seasons

fall

As the evenings draw in, it's time to start making your home all cozy (*koselig* in Norwegian or *hugnaligt* in Faroese). Get your candles, blankets, and sheepskins out and create more *mys* (warmth and comfort).

This might also be the time to start on that knitting project. Guðrun Rógvadóttir, one of the founders of the knitwear company Gudrun and Gudrun, and also the creator of the famous sweaters from the Danish TV series *The Killing*, says that knitting is huge in the Faroe Islands: "We spend a lot of time indoors in the colder months so knitting is a way of just being at home whilst also creating something." She added that knitting is a kind of "meditative process, a way of slowing down... We get a lot of orders from Japan and they are not only buying a jumper, they are also buying the idea of the time it took to knit the garment."

Here are some ways that you can adapt to and embrace this season in your home.

- **Crafting:** Start on a simple knitting project—something that you can pick up without having to think a lot about the next step.

- **Flowers and plants:** Make simple fall flower arrangements and plant things such as ornamental cabbage, heather, and ivy.

- **Seasonal decorations:** Decorate your home with colorful fall leaves, small pumpkins, and twig wreaths.

winter

The most noticeable change in Winter is that in many countries the evenings start earlier. Even though it happens at the same time each year, that blanket of darkness seems to "arrive" out of nowhere, almost by surprise. While Christmas and Advent are bright spots in the gloomy winter calendar, November can drag out as it doesn't have much seasonal celebration to look forward to.

Many Nordics use the cold and dark season as a reason to gather together, eat seasonal and special foods, and make our homes as warm and bright as the outside is dark and cold. Here are three easy ways that you can create some Nordic cheer in the darkest of seasons.

tea and treats

Invite your friends for *fika* (see page 116) and serve some home-baked gingerbread, a Swedish *lussebulle* (a sweet saffron bun), or as they do in Denmark, *aebleskiver*, which is a spherical round pancake. Alternatively, instead of coffee or tea, you could make some piping hot mulled wine—*glögg* in Swedish and Icelandic, *gløgg* in Danish and Norwegian, or *glögi* in Finnish.

106 the nordic home

window decorations

A couple of lights in the window are great for bringing cheer to passersby and creating that warm and cozy, or as the Swedes would say *mysig*, atmosphere. Try a traditional electric seven-arm advent light, a string of fairy lights, or a hanging star made from paper, straw, or metal with a light in it. The Nordics traditionally hang star decorations in their windows, perhaps because we feel close to the stars during the long winter nights.

candles

Get a set of four advent candles and light the first of four candles on the fourth Sunday before Christmas. Light a new candle each Sunday before Christmas, so that by Christmas Eve all four candles are lit. It's traditional to dress your candle holders with some greenery—you could use moss, branches of pine, and small pinecones.

living with the seasons 107

christmas

Christmas is the brightest shining star in the Nordic winter calendar. Many of the Nordics celebrate it in a similar way, although there are variations from country to country. For example, most Nordic countries celebrate on 24th December and have one Santa bringing the presents but in Iceland, they have 13 *Jólasveinar* (Yule lads) instead. They start delivering little gifts to children from the 12th up to *Jól* (Christmas Eve) on the 24th December.

Throughout the Nordic countries, homes get increasingly decorated with lots of natural materials that not only give a beautiful scent, but also add a lovely element to the décor. The Nordics see Christmas as not just one day but several small moments and celebrations. Try adding in something festive here and there, such as foods with traditional and warming spices and flavors. Don't get carried away by the in-your-face commercialism displayed by supermarkets and big shops. Focus on simplicity and natural decorations, scents, and flavors.

108 the nordic home

- **Winter flowers:** Plant traditional winter bulbs in pots in early to mid-winter, so that by the time the darkest season rolls around they are out in bloom and make your house smell amazing. I like using hyacinths, amaryllis, and paperwhites.

- **Festive candles:** Take some small offcuts from your Christmas tree, attach them to an empty jar with twine or ribbon, and place a tea light inside.

- **Citrus ornaments:** Cut oranges into slices, dry them in the oven at 350°F (70°C) for 2–3 hours, and use wire or thread to string them up as a garland.

- **Pine decorations:** Use branches of pine to make wreaths or pop them in a rustic jar as a mini Christmas tree. Add eucalyptus for a more spicy scent.

- **Snow-cleaned rugs:** In this old tradition, you hang your rugs outside so they get cold, then lay them out on the ground and cover each one with dry (not-about-to-melt) snow. Let them sit for a few minutes, then brush off the snow. This gives your rugs a crisp, newly washed smell.

the importance of an open window

Looking out of a window and receiving light through it are both valuable, easy actions to take to improve our physical, psychological, and maybe even spiritual well-being, but the benefits multiply when we open those windows. Take vitamin D, for example. One of the best ways to get vitamin D is through exposure to sunlight, since the sun emits ultraviolet waves that set off a chemical reaction when they reach the skin, creating vitamin D. But the important thing is that although sunshine can pass through glass, the ultraviolet waves cannot, so if you want to increase your intake of vitamin D, sit by an open window where possible.

Plus, there is more to an open window than vitamin absorption. When you were a child and your mom told you to go outside and get some fresh air, she was onto something—a study published in the journal *Indoor Air* found that in ventilated spaces where the air circulates there is less carbon dioxide buildup. Lower carbon dioxide levels in the air around us lead to deeper, longer, and less interrupted sleep. Our bodies don't have to work so hard to do their jobs of cleansing our cells, lungs, and blood, and so we can better settle and rest.

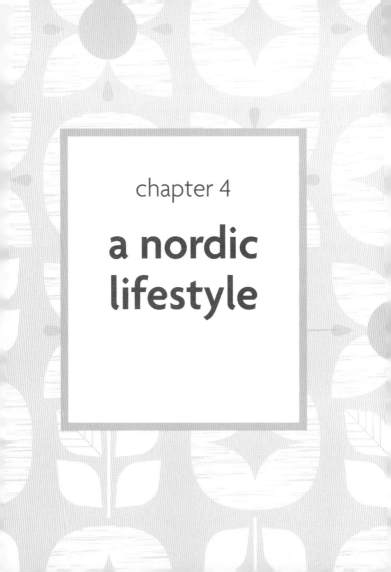

chapter 4
a nordic lifestyle

finding happiness the nordic way

A study done in Berkeley, California, found that people who prioritized happiness felt lonelier on a daily basis than those who didn't concentrate on it, as assessed through diary entries made over two weeks. If you have a preformed idea of what happiness should feel like, there is a big chance that when something good actually happens, not only do you not feel as happy as expected, but you may also feel disappointed.

Instead, Nordics find contentment by enjoying the small pleasures in life. Having a special corner in your garden or in a natural space near your home, where you can sit and relax during the day without too much fuss. Discovering a local walk where you can observe nature's changes throughout the year. Even something small, such as making a hot drink in your favorite mug with some loose-leaf tea and a strainer.

fika

"fee-ka" • Swedish • noun
A break for coffee and something sweet, where you can slow down and savor the good things in life.

fika moments

Fika is a pretty established concept in Sweden. After *tack* (thank you or please) and *hej* (hello), it's the most important word to learn. It's a break for coffee and a sweet treat, such as cookies or cake, similar to Finland's *pullakahvi* (coffee and a bun). The sweet treat can come from a packet or be homemade—Swedish recipes tend to balance difficulty and ease so recipes are neither too hard nor too simple, the ingredients can all go in one bowl, and you can always take an *ögonmått* (basically, measurement by eye).

Most Swedes take *fika* every day, several times a day, with friends, family, or colleagues. The breaks don't take up too much of your time but will be long enough to talk about the main things on your mind, which can be anything from family events to work-related issues (but not in the office). Anything not covered you can talk about next time. The importance of *fika* lies in having a break and being together—if we don't stop, we just keep going and going. *Fika* has become a way to define any switch-off moment, when you step away from a busy and hectic world.

the nordic diet

While the Nordics enjoy their sweet treats, their diet is generally about eating whole, unprocessed foods, with an emphasis on mindfulness and an absence of stress around mealtimes. It consists of locally sourced and seasonal produce, and ingredients that are high in nutrients.

Nordic meals contain lots of fruit, berries, seasonal vegetables, wholegrains—the Nordics love their bread—and of course plenty of fish and dairy. The Nordic diet is also very much based around salted, cured, pickled, and fermented foods, due to the weather and the long cold season when it's not possible to grow or pick fresh foods.

Planning, shopping, and cooking can be overwhelming, but sticking to whole food ingredients, following what's in season, and knowing a handful of simple recipes that you can repeat weekly is key to a good Nordic diet. You can also make any meal more well-rounded by adding a few candles to your table and dishing up extra plates of raw vegetables and crackerbread with butter.

nourish yourself with good food

Diet culture is everywhere today, and it's not uncommon to have lots of rules about what we should and shouldn't eat, putting food into categories of "good" or "bad." However, quite often going on a strict diet with the aim of only losing weight can deprive you of important food groups. Food should not only feed our hunger but on a deeper level also bring us joy and nourishment in equal measure.

Instead, try eating with the seasons—it's good for the environment, your bank balance, and your body, too. Buy in bulk and freeze, pickle, or make preserves. Keep a few simple, good ingredients at hand, and a few basic recipes up your sleeve, to help minimize stress. Grow some herbs—they will really add zing to your cooking. Basil, oregano, chives, and parsley are as happy on a sunny windowsill as they are outside. Just make sure to cut them before they bloom for more flavor.

sustainable skincare

Nordics take the same attitude to nourishing their skin as they do with their food—natural, locally sourced ingredients you cannot find elsewhere. Think extracts from marine algae, nourishing tree sap, and antioxidant-rich berries. In order to endure conditions so far north, plants must adapt their defenses—making for more potent ingredients. This means that your skincare routine can be minimalistic and yet very effective.

A lot of new Nordic beauty brands also focus on using sustainable ingredients and environmentally friendly packaging, reducing the impact on the planet. This comes from a deep respect for and connection to nature. Laura Heikkilä, the founder of Finnish skincare company Nörre Nordic, says, "The rest of the world can certainly learn from the Scandi approach to skincare, as it emphasizes the importance of taking care of one's skin in a natural and sustainable way. By using locally sourced and minimally processed ingredients, Nordic skincare has a lower environmental impact while delivering effective results."

create a daily routine

When it comes to products, I find that less is definitely more. Use a gentle cleanser in the evening that doesn't disrupt the skin's barrier; I like the oil-cleansing method in the colder months. Then apply a simple plant-based oil such as jojoba or a serum, or nothing at all. In the morning, depending on the season and your skin type, wash only with water, followed by a tallow-based cream or a light lotion to moisturize.

If you are healthy, your skin looks at its best. Look after yourself and increase your knowledge about what makes you feel good in terms of food, exercise, spending time outside, simple skincare, and enjoyment. Make a plan with a vision about what you believe a happy, balanced life should be. At the same time, be patient as nothing happens overnight, and embrace aging by focusing on staying strong and healthy.

sustainable skincare **127**

mysa

"mee-sa" • Swedish • verb

Taking time out from stress and doing something that makes you feel cozy and comfortable, like seeing friends or sitting in front of a toasty fireplace.

koselig

"koosh-lee" • Norwegian • noun
A sense of coziness, warmth, and happiness that can be achieved no matter the weather by staying connected with others.

the nordic approach to relationships

We all know that spending quality time with other people is important for our mental and spiritual health, but it's also important to do it in the right way. When you grow up in a large family, negotiating in a kind way and considering other people's feelings is the key to ensuring everyone can get along. You would never dream of taking the last cookie on the plate. If there are not enough for everyone to have seconds, what is left will be divided up. This comes as second nature and, in a way, is how Swedish society functions as a whole.

Competition and rivalry in all its manifestations are usually put forward positively as healthy and developmental for the majority of individuals and society. However, in the book *Klara Färdiga Gå* (*Ready, Steady, Go*), Eva-Lotta Hulten explores the idea that competition can be harmful, and acting as rivals can leave us beset by feelings of worthlessness and loneliness. Instead, Swedish people prioritize showing compassion for their fellow man and I think that is what's needed right now in the world, and what many people are striving for. I believe it can ultimately make you happier.

132 a nordic lifestyle

connect with your loved ones

So often we think we are paying attention, or making ourselves understood, when the opposite is true. When we tune in to what people are really saying, we feel more strongly connected and more compassionate. When we feel heard and understood we feel more loved, better supported, more contented, and we are more likely to listen to and help others. As the saying goes: you have one mouth and two ears—make sure you listen twice as much as you speak!

Similarly, getting physical with someone else—through hugs, holding hands, or even sitting close together in front of a cozy fire—reduces your stress levels and increases your body's production of oxytocin, a "happy" hormone. This makes you feel happier, and will also boost your immune system. Simply showing your friends and family physical affection will make everyone a little bit healthier and more content.

socialize only as much as you need

To say that you are *utbränd*, or burned out, is socially accepted by the people in many Nordic countries, who as a general rule don't display a lot of emotions. Michelle Baker, a New Yorker living in Sweden who teaches yoga and breathwork, says she had never heard of this concept before she arrived in Sweden. She says that "Summers in Sweden are intense, people have lots of time off, but no one makes time for yoga and relaxation and as a result, they come back in the fall totally exhausted and at the point of burn out."

It's a case of knowing when to stop and not going overboard, realizing when you are actually content and not going after more, which is a natural thing for human beings to do but doesn't always lead to more happiness. Ask yourself if your week has a good balance of activities and commitments. Perhaps you could arrange your social life differently. A big party is not necessary for happiness but having a hot drink with a friend could do it. A book club is a good example of a balanced activity as you meet friends and enjoy socializing at someone's house, but you also spend time reading.

the nordic approach to relationships 135

kura skymning

"cure-ah-skim-ning" • Swedish • verb
The act of sitting quietly and pondering at dusk. It involves simply slowing down at the end of a hectic day, reflecting, and taking in the natural beauty.

conclusion

Despite all the benefits of the Nordic way of life, it's clear there are still some things that aren't perfect— the Nordic countries have their fair share of issues with mental health like any other. However, perhaps because of that, we can gain wisdom from how they tackle those issues and manage stress and overwhelm in this increasingly crazy and busy world.

When we are stuck in a worried mode, doing things that could improve our lives can lead to feelings of guilt because many of us associate personal care with self-indulgence and shame. But living well isn't about things that are grand, wild, and spectacular or cost money. By truthfully examining what you really need— peace, calm, and connection, and less distraction and stress—you can affect where your attention goes and do things that improve your wellbeing without you even having to add it to your to-do list.

making small changes

Take inspiration from the vast open spaces of the north, the dense forests, high mountains, and freshwater lakes and rivers, where you can find joy in eating berries straight off the bush that have been warmed by the sun, or forage for mushrooms and cook them outside. Pare down your stuff—not only products you use for your skin and body but also things in your home—to reflect nature, where less is more and just *being* is enough.

Teach yourself resilience, because it's easy to postpone "connecting with nature" outside on a gray, cold day in the winter until a sunny day comes around. Living seasonally and focusing on the possibilities rather than on the limitations of the weather is something that the Nordics do well, because there is beauty in the flow of a storm and the short days, just as there is in all seasons of life.

Learn how to love your home even more and create a place that makes you feel truly relaxed. Most people would probably admit that staying in is a bit of a luxury, so if you're not going out, make sure your home works for you, is inviting, has lots of living plants, and helps you feel cozy and safe. Your home is a reflection of you, and it should be just how you like it without being a slave to what other people think.

And, finally, take pleasure in small luxuries. Time spent with friends and family. Those breaks for *fika* and good conversation. Decorating your windowsill with plants. Sitting in a warm ray of sun. Cooking seasonal comfort foods. Knitting some socks. Hunkering down in front of a good movie for some *fredagsmys* (cozy Friday nights in). By assigning time to the things we really value in life, which make us happy, we can achieve more balance and find joy in every day.

conclusion **141**

resources

Scandinavia Standard—one-stop info for all Scandiphiles
scandinaviastandard.com

The Swedish Society for Nature Conservation
naturskyddsforeningen.se

Visit Norway
visitnorway.com

Visit Finland
visitfinland.com

Swedish Tourist Association
swedishtouristassociation.com

Visit Iceland
visiticeland.com

Visit Denmark
visitdenmark.com

Faroe Islands Tourist Board
faroeislands.fo

Nordic Walking
nordicwalking.co.uk

further reading

The Lagom Life: A Swedish Way of Living by Elisabeth Carlsson (CICO Books, 2023)

The Book of Nordic Self-care : Find Peace and Balance Through Seasonal Rituals, Connecting with Nature, Mindfulness Practices, and More by Elisabeth Carlsson (CICO Books, 2023)

The Open-Air Life: Discover the Nordic Art of Friluftsliv and Embrace Nature Every Day by Linda Åkeson McGurk (TarcherPerigee, 2022)

The Sustainable Home: Easy Ways to Live with Nature in Mind by Ida Magntorn (Pavilion Books, 2022)

Döstädning: The Gentle Art of Swedish Death Cleaning by Margareta Magnusson (Canongate Books, 2020)

Sisu: The Finnish Art of Courage by Joanna Nylund (Gaia, 2018)

picture credits

t = top; b = bottom; bg = background

© AdobeStock.com
mindfullness: graphics throughout; **Adrian:** page 2; **Roxana:** pages 6–7;
orangeberry: backgrounds on pages 10–11, 20–21, 32–33, 74–75, 76–77,
94–95, 112–113, 134–135; **somchai20162516:** pages 14–15 bg; **venis:** page 17;
ImagePulse: page 21; **Geber86:** pages 22–23; **Sergii Mostovyi:** page 26;
Juhku: pages 26–27 bg, 50–51 bg; **Stephanie Frey:** page 27; **progressman:**
page 31; **Florian Kunde:** page 34; **avtk:** page 37; **StellaSalander:** page 38;
AllThings: page 41 t; **Ed:** page 41 b; **JFL Photography:** page 42; **misign:**
page 47; **Lars Johansson:** pages 50, 116–117 bg; **LumineImages:** page 55;
Per: page 57; **sokko_natalia:** page 59; **pierrick:** page 60;
visualspectrum/Stocksy: page 61; **Alena Ozerova:** page 62; **tramper79:**
page 63; **nyul:** page 66; **nicoletaionescu:** page 68; **terovesalainen:** pages
68–69 bg; **Tracy Ben:** page 71; **Galina Zhigalova:** page 75; **lukaPixMedia:**
pages 80–81 bg; **Lasvu:** page 83; **FollowTheFlow:** pages 90–91; **maxcity:**
page 93; **Nidai:** page 94; **Pixel Skull Design:** pages 96–97 bg;
beataaldridge: page 99; **Maren Winter:** page 107; **Alexandra:** page 114;
Pixel-Shot: page 123; **Social Material:** page 127; **DisobeyArt:** pages
128–129; **Nina L/peopleimages.com:** page 131; **Suzi Media:** page 132;
Anna: page 135; **gdefilip:** pages 136–137 bg; **Aleksei Potov:** pages 138–139

© Ryland Peters & Small
Debi Treloar: pages 9, 12, 18, 88; **Elisabeth Carlsson:** pages 14, 64, 67;
Mark Scott: pages 24, 84; **Catherine Gratwicke:** pages 78, 97, 101; **Joanna
Henderson:** page 80; **James Merrell:** page 87; **Peter Cassidy:** pages 102,
119, 140; **Martin Norris:** page 105; **Caroline Arber:** page 108; **Jan Baldwin:**
pages 111, 139; **Steve Painter:** page 116

acknowledgments

A huge thank you to my beautiful children, Alvar, Clara, and Iris, and my husband Oliver. You mean everything to me. Love always.

My mom and my dad for showing me love through seasonal traditions and food, dragging me out for woodland foraging walks, and creating a stable and warm family environment full of *fika* moments.

My wonderful family in Sweden for inspiration, for advice, and for generally being a really great bunch.

CICO Books—Carmel, Sally, Emily, Patricia, Danielle—for giving me the chance to make another book, and Geoff Borin for his design.

The many people who gave up their time to chat to me and share their valuable perspective on many things. In no particular order: Anne, Anja, Tiina, Michelle, Pia, Thorgerdur Anna, Gunnar, Marika, Richard, Gudrun, Peter, Miles, Lena, Sanna, Kari, Helga, Tanja, Thommy, Linn, Anna-Karin, and Susanna.

And Ella—our Cavapoo who always waits so patiently for her walks.